One morning in September Jelly woke up before Bean. He was snoring in the corner of the shed. Jelly went out of the door quietly.

She went across the farmyard and under the gate without Wellington or Kevin seeing her. Both dogs were fast asleep on the floor of the kennel.

Jelly went down the lane. She heard the birds tweeting to each other. Then she heard another noise. "Toot, toot." It was the horn of the farmer's van.

The van came around the corner very fast. Jelly quickly jumped out of the way, and the van just missed her. She fell among the thorns of a blackberry bush.

The van went on its way to the farm.
The farmer had not even seen Jelly.
Meanwhile, she was stuck among the
thorns of the blackberry bush.

She tried to move, but the thorns dug into her. The more she moved, the more they hurt her. She was trapped in them.

Then she heard another noise. It was a sort of screeching noise. Jelly looked down the lane. Oh no! It was the big white goose.

Jelly was more afraid of the goose than the thorns. She pulled herself free, and she limped back to the farmyard.

She crept into the shed and lay down on the floor. She felt worn out. Poor Jelly! She was licking herself when she saw Bean looking at her.

"Good morning," he said. Jelly did not reply. She did not think it was a "good" morning. It was a "bad" morning, and she started to cry. Poor Jelly!

"or"   "ore"   "oor"

morning	before
for	more
or	snoring
horn	
sort	door
corner	floor
thorns	poor
worn	